**LETTERS
SO
THAT
HAPPINESS**

Letters So That Happiness
Copyright © 2018 by the Estate of Arnaldo Calveyra
Translation copyright © 2018 by Elizabeth Zuba

This translation is based on *Cartas para que la alegría*
(Cooperativa Impresora y Distribuidora, Buenos Aires, 1959)

Lost Literature Series #22

ISBN 978-1-946433-05-3
First Edition, First Printing, 2018
Edition of 1,000

Ugly Duckling Presse
The Old American Can Factory
232 Third Street #E-303
Brooklyn, NY 11215
www.uglyducklingpresse.org

Distributed in the USA by Small Press Distribution
Distributed in Canada via Coach House Books
by Raincoast Books
Distributed in the UK by Inpress Books

Design and typesetting by Doormouse
Covers printed letterpress at Ugly Duckling Presse
Interiors printed offset and bound at McNaughton & Gunn

Work published within the framework of "Sur" Translation Support Program of the Ministry of Foreign Affairs, International Trade and Worship of the Argentine Republic. Obra editada en el marco del Programa "Sur" de Apoyo a las Traducciones del Ministerio de Relaciones Exteriores y Culto de la República Argentina.

This book was made possible in part by a grant from the National Endowment for the Arts and by public funds from the New York City Department of Cultural Affairs in partnership with the City Council; the translation was supported by the New York State Council on the Arts.

Letters So That Happiness

Arnaldo Calveyra

translated from the Spanish
by Elizabeth Zuba

Lost Literature Series #22
Ugly Duckling Presse
Brooklyn, NY

Letters So That Happiness

El viaje lo trajimos lo mejor que se pudo. De todas las mariposas de alfalfa que nos siguieron desde Mansilla, la última se rezagó en Desvío Clé. Nos acompañamos ese trecho, ella con el volar y yo con la mirada. Venía con las alas de amarillo adiós, y, de tanto agitarse contra el aire, ya no alegraba una mariposa sino que una fuente ardía. Y corrió todavía con las alas de echar el resto: una mirada también ardiendo paralela al no puedo más en el costado de tren que siguió.

La gallina que me diste la compartí con Rosa, ella me dio budín. En tren es casi lo que andar en mancarrón.

Los que tocaban guitarra cuando me despedías vinieron alegres hasta Buenos Aires.

Casi a mediodía entró el guarda con paso de "aquí van a suceder cosas", y hubo que ocultar a cuanta cotorra o pollo vivo inocente de Dios se estaba alimentando.

En el ferry fue tan lindo mirar el agua.

¿Y sabes?, no supe que estaba triste hasta que me pidieron que cantara.

The journey, we brought it along the best we could. Of all the alfalfa butterflies that followed from Mansilla, it was the last one that lingered at Desvío Clé. We took that stretch together, she with flying and me with a gaze. She came with wings of goodbye yellow, and with so much beating against the air, she ceased gladdening, butterfly, and burned a fountain. And still she ran with her wings to shake off the wreckage: a second gaze burning parallel to the I just can't anymore from the side of the train it followed.

The chicken you gave me, I shared it with Rosa, she gave me sweet bread. By train is almost like going by donkey.

The guys playing guitar when you saw me off played happily 'til Buenos Aires.

Just before noon, the guard came through with a saunter of "things are really gonna start happening around here," and everyone had to hide any live innocent before God parrots or chickens they were feeding.

On the ferry, it was beautiful looking out at the water.

And you know? I didn't know I was sad until they asked me to sing.

La casita se ha convertido en algo cerca del mar. Un olor que penetraba desde temprano por las maderillas, el seguro del viento: en las más altas ramas de todo; su ajetreo de venir de un agua, es decir, el cambio de la ola en viento cuando ya no puede más que esos pocos metros sobre la playa.

Y ahora que ya es de noche, estoy contento de parecerme al mar, y caigo también sobre la hoja con este hermoso destino de continuar ese mar y este viento y tocar el poblado allá en la guardia inquietada de los álamos.

The house has turned into something near the sea. A smell that slipped early through the wooden slats, the wind's latch: in the highest branches of all; the bustle of coming from water, that is, the change from wave to wind when it just can't much more those few meters of beach.

And now that it's night, I'm happy to be like the sea, and fall too over a leaf with this beautiful charge of continuing that sea and this wind and touching the village over there past the restless poplar guards.

No te dije de la luna. La luna es lo más alto. Cuando la mirábamos, ¿por qué hacíamos retemblar el índice sobre el labio hasta provocar un beruberu de acompañarla? ¿Nos lo enseñaste tú o papá? ¿Y qué era su despabilarse en niño Jesús subido al burrito sobre esa lumbre de peligro? Dame esas noticias. Nos quedábamos hasta bien tarde en enero para mirar. Ahí la tengo en el patio ahora, es lo más alto. La dejé atada del pino, mi cometa plateada y mi compaña, y me entré luna arriba para que muchos niños.

I didn't tell you about the moon. The moon is the highest thing. Why, when we looked up, did we let our fingers tremble at our lips until the bababa went up to join it? Did you teach us that or papa? And what was it quickening in baby Jesus up on the donkey over that blazing peril? Tell me that news. We stayed until late January to look up. I have it there now, in the backyard, it's the highest thing. I left it tied to the pine tree, my silver kite and my company, and I went upmoon so that all the children.

Ya van para veinte años en el color del fierro.

Recuerdo la cocina en el hervor del frío de bolsillos y la boca en el humo cantando del buen día.

El gato o el fogón rumiando hasta no entenderlas, las palabras de arar, o de moler el maíz, o de ir al pueblo, y la taza ávida y bocona probando antes que nadie el sabor del candeal, y la escarcha de rocío coloreando la teja hasta la gota.

Cuando tocabas la campana ya algún muchachito viejo viruejo de picopicotuejo de pomporerá enfilaba por la calle de los paraísos. Eso parecía bastarte, te sacabas el delantal del desayuno y el menudo blanco redondeando en las rodillas de tu guardapolvo se alejaba unos pasos.

¿Y de cómo nos repartías el amor no te acuerdas?, ¿de cómo no cambiaba el descanso de tu rostro en el día de campanada subiendo?, ¿de cómo no cambiaba el azul de tu encontrada cuando ibas con todos nosotros al buen día del aula?

They're already going on twenty in the color of iron.

I remember the kitchen in the boil of cold pockets and the mouth in the steam singing good morning.

The cat or the stove ruminating so much you couldn't catch them, the plowing words, or grinding corn words, or going to the village words, and the eager and huge mouth cup before anyone else tasting the sweet *candeal*, and the frost coloring in the tile right up to the trickle.

When you rang the bell, some little boy blue go blow your horn was already heading down Paradise Way. That seemed about right, and you took off your breakfast apron and the faded white rounded at the knees of your overalls distanced itself a few paces.

And how you handed out your love to us, don't you remember? how the quiet of your face never changed through the climbing bell day? how your finding blue never changed when you went with us to the good morning of the classroom?

Soñé con la casa color de tormenta. Estaba yo conmigo una mañana de 1943. A las ventanas se remansaba el balcón esperándolo todo. Estaba descalzo, con la luz que me hacía cosquillas para que saliera de ella, y el sol no estaba a las baldosas sino que ya era en el río de dos riberas. En una, yo. En la de sombra, si se la miraba a los ojos, retumbaban nuestras voces hacia el fulgor de remos en el pasar azul. Y de nuevo era en el patio que estrellaba naranja en instante de cascotazo entero sobre cachurra monta la burra y el finado Urquiza como el ánima del rey del Hamlet les arengaba in hoc signo vinces en la respuesta agorrionada.

Yo hubiera querido esa poca luz pasando a la altura de los ojos pero alguien murmuró que igualmente había que encenderla, y me levantaron de cabezal de agua y se bailaba con una soledad de la isla jacarandá.

"Tienes que amar mucho", me dijo la rama. "¿Y esto?", le dije, y no pude sino despertarme.

Era la rama con la luz.

I dreamed about the storm-colored house. I was there with myself one morning in 1943. The balcony pooled at the windows waiting for everything. I was barefoot, with a light that tickled at me so I would run from it and the sun wasn't on the tiles anymore but always already in the double-banked river. Me, on the one side. On the shaded side, if you looked it in the eyes, our voices thundered toward the radiance of oars in the blue passing. And then on the patio again blowing up instantly orange pelting hard over leap-frog and the late Urquiza like the king's soul in Hamlet urging in hoc signo vinces in its sparrowed reply.

I would've wanted that little light passing by at eye level but someone muttered you'd have to light it just the same, and lifted my head from the water headboard and danced with the loneliness of the jacaranda island.

"You have to love a lot," said the branch. "And this?" I said, and all I could do was wake up.

It was the branch with the light.

Un galope abría ramadas hacia el este de las tunas; no podíamos saber quién era, qué era, tan así, tan a campo traviesa; y luego, los perros, todos, que ladraban y parecían acometer algo de bulto por su furia momentáneamente ensimismada. Apagamos la luz porque la luna. Y por más que escudriñábamos, se ahogaba ese no saber en la blancura extrema sobre el campo. Papá dijo que las gallinas; a mí me apagaste una suposición con un "no será nada"; pero antes de que él saliera con la escopeta ya volvías de las piezas del frente diciéndole que era Billín, nuestro hermano.

Y ya no te vi sino cuando apareciste de entre los ligustros, con los botines embarrados, del tajamar esplendente, con él por delante, retrasándote, tú retrasándote para que te copiara la suavidad del paso y no se nos despertara en el pie del sueño, hasta que se entró en la cama.

A gallop parted the branches to the east of the prickly pears; we couldn't have known who it was, what it was, so much like this, so much through the field; and later, the dogs, all of them, that barked and seemed to mob some shape with some momentary spellbound fury. We turned off the lights because the moon. And for all we searched, that not-knowing kept drowning in the far white out over the field. Papa said that the chickens; you turned out my fear with an "it won't be anything;" but before he could leave with his rifle you had already come back saying it was Billín, our brother.

And I couldn't see you until you came up through the wild privet, your boots all muddied from the resplendent creek water, he ahead of you, keeping you from gaining, you yourself keeping yourself from gaining so that he would mirror your gentle gait and we wouldn't wake at the foot of his dream until he got back into bed.

Kikirikí grita una hierba entre los dos pulgares.
¡Mira hasta qué lejos el yuyal se encresta!
No es el aire que pasaba, no. Ni el andador de loma que se ensaya a solas a no voltear los niños.
Y las cañas locas por la música y el silbido de la perdiz que le contestan, ¡cómo se esconden y en el eco de vuelta se dislocan, suben!
¡Mira hasta qué arriba en la veleta la cresta colorada del kikirikí!

Cockledoodledoo whoops a blade of grass between two thumbs.

Look how far out the high weeds crest!

It isn't the air that wended, no. Or the hill-walker practicing not flipping the children over.

And the music-crazy reeds and the partridge's whistle that answers back: how they hide and then dislocate and rise in the return echo!

Look, the red crest of the cockledoodledoo way up in the weathervane!

Como si estuviera por llegarme a cada instante esta compaña de siempre, en la cueva del invierno de una friolera, junto al perro que encontramos en tu día, subo a la loma que se apura a que yo regrese para darte las margaritas alegres.

Es gozosa la llegada de pulmones, gritarte que asomes con tu falda de patatas a ponderar flores y mandarlas en seguida a los santos.

Y después era día de otras cosas, y a una hora de ese día nos dábamos cuenta de que no sería tampoco tu día, de que no cumplirías años.

¡Pero qué alegre ademán la biznaga ardiendo, y ponerse en cuclillas el sol, y abanico de lámpara, y recordar versos de memoria, y tu niñez de nosotros desde nuestras espaldas como el estante más alto sobre puntas de pie abuelita qué horas son, en tu homenaje!

En este día de seguida con sol alto de invierno me quedo aquí oyéndote la mañana que me trajiste a lomas, a desniveles de aguas, el otro cumpleaños de los dos.

As if it were ever almost here this forever company in the cave of a shiverer's winter, together with the dog we found on your day, I jump up on the hill that hurries to take me back to bring you happy daisies.

It's wonderful the coming of lungs, yelling for you to come out with your potato skirt to praise the flowers and send them right off to the saints.

And later it was a day of other things, and at some point that day we realized it wouldn't be your day either, that you wouldn't turn a year older.

But what a happy gesture the burning bishop's weed, and the sun's crouching, and fanning out lamplight, and recalling verses by heart, and your childhood of us above us like the highest shelf on tiptoes Grandma what time is it, in your honor!

On this long single day with winter's high sun I hear you here the morning you brought me to hills, to declivities of water, the other birthday of both.

La muchachita guardapolvo blanco venía a la cocina a darnos el buen día, no esperaba la campanada de entrar al aula.

Una mañana me encontró llorando, y me di vuelta para que no viera lo que lloraba. Ella se apuró en la mentira hasta el punto porque otras niñas andaban por ahí con miradas de irse sacándonos la lengua.

Tenía la facilidad de subirse a la cara las margaritas silvestres sin arrancarlas, ¿no recordarías su nombre?

White overalls girl came into the kitchen to wish us good morning, she didn't wait for the classroom bell.

One morning she saw me crying and I turned so she wouldn't see what I cried. She hurried straight through to the end of that lie because there were other girls around giving us stick-our-tongues-out-at-you looks.

She had a talent for lifting wild daisies to her cheek without ever picking them, you wouldn't remember her name?

El muchacho volvía por lo confiado de la noche. El servicio militar le había enseñado a robar y a silbar por cualquier cosa. Ahora, de robar se olvidaba silbando. Las casuarinas emplumadas se aquietaban a su paso. Pero como no conocen el tiempo que va de una tristeza a una alegría, no hubo viento que despertara a los nidos dormidos en su puño: para ellas, él volvía, una de tantas, del poblado.

Y él silbaba para las casuarinas emplumadas, y para la noche rebelde a la luz mala, y para la estrella, allá en la copa de la ligustra de Zumino.

Cuando se acercaba a la casa lo engatusó un aire de armónica, y dejó de silbar. La madre estaba ocupada en la cocina, y el valse rengueaba desde la pieza contigua hasta entablar un contrapunto con la chispa de diablo. El soldadito se quedó otro instante en el anticipo, y le parecía oírlo del revés. La vislumbre del cuarto le lamía los botines. Entonces, levantó las piernas de trepar ventanas, trepó la ventana y se entró en el valse.

¿No lo recuerdas?, era Orlando, cuando volvió del servicio militar.

The boy came back by the mettle of the night. The military had taught him to steal and whistle for anything. Now whistling he forgot stealing. Feathered casuarina trees quieted to his step. But because they'd never met the winds that travel from a sadness to a happiness, there was no breeze to wake the nests sleeping in their fist: for them, he was returning, one of so many from the village.

And he whistled for the feathered casuarinas, and for the rebel night to the phantom light, and for the star there at the top of Zumino's wild privet.

As he neared the house, a harmonica wind lured him along, and he stopped whistling. The mother was busy in the kitchen and a waltz limped from the adjoining room until it fell counterpoint with the devil's spark. The soldier lingered there a moment in the wings, it was like hearing it all inside out. The room's haziest glimmer licking his boots. Then he lifted his climbing-window legs, climbed the window and entered the waltz.

Don't you remember? it was Orlando, when he got back from the service.

Ya limpio de la honda y de la piedra salí a mirar otoño de la variación. En lo escampado de la loma sube y baja el camaleón herido por aguas bebiéndose a sí mismas.

Otoño ancas partidas ya le ganaba al día entumecido de alabar de junto al pozo. Las puertas de barro cocido del verano cayendo en el escobazo de la hojarasca.

Aire bajo en bamboleo un momento. Y quiero retruco de los cañaverales en contragolpe y al remanso.

Pampero cuacuá desde los juncos de paso. Y degollado en mi cabeza de nidal de carancho, ¿y cómo están los ríos por allá?, ¿el grano de descarte destetando ratones acaso?

La primera sobrevenida sin tu mano del cementerio. Y volví al galope con perradas en mi sombra — y el cañadón retacón que me daba una luz de ventaja. Pero todavía subiendo en loma hasta la nube corderito: allí se llenaba la luna, sobre el horizonte que se derrumbaba achatando al lechuzón soltero. Y adiós colores demorados al fondo de verdes y agua zaina de potros con ansias de potros.

Pampero patas frías.

Porque la noche.

Clean free of the sling and stone I went out to watch the autumn of the variation. On the hillside, the chameleon rises and falls harrowed by the water that drinks the water.

Chapped haunches autumn already beating out the day numb from praise at the well. Summer's fired mud doors falling into the broom thwack of dead leaves.

Low air staggering a moment. And I raise the bet on the reedbeds' counter, counterlash and to the stillwater.

Pampero winds quack-quack in the through-rush. And throat-slit in my falcon nesting box head, and how are the rivers over there? the grain from the chaff weaning the mice maybe?

The first come up without your hand from the grave. And I went back to a gallop with the herd dogs in my shadow — and the lean ravine that gave me an edge of light. But still heading up the hill toward the little lamb cloud: there where the moon filled up over the crumbling horizon flattening the only owl. And good-bye late colors at the depths of greens and the colt-shadowed water waiting for the colts.

Pampero winds cold feet.

Because the night.

De pronto, ¡qué alegría! Venía mirando por el otoño suelto y me entretuve en un cardo, junto al tobogán estancado de hojarasca. ¡Curioso!, estaba florecido de recién y se entró en la leche cruda. Yo me salí corriendo de su costado en trance, de su ebriedad silenciosa me fui lejos con los perros; "ya está ya está"... y nosotros, y el azúcar despertado y los panes convidados al festejo.

Y ya está en cuajada ahora, tan blanco, tan de una florecida de blanco puro, el azul.

Me entré tranquilamente al cardo cimarrón, querida mamá.

Suddenly, how wonderful! I came looking through loose autumn and slowed to a thistle beside the slide piled high with dead leaves. Wild! recently bloomed and gone into the raw milk. I went out running from its side in a trance, from its silent drunkenness I went off with the dogs; "it's here, it's here" ... and us and the woken sugar and the breads shared in the celebration.

And now it's already curded, so white, so much a flourish of pure white, the blue.

I went calmly into the wild thistle, mama.

El globo que nos trajeron las visitas de Buenos Aires, ¡qué lástima que se fue!

Tanto que por la noche antes le preparamos el cordel de la subida con cuanta piola encontramos viva o muerta para volverlo una cometa azul a la mañana.

Viró al costado del naranjo con el patio, hizo un esfuerzo por el aire y aguantó la luz.

¿Subía?

Viró hacia el sur donde ralean las cañas y las gallinas se asustan de solas. Le vimos el esfuerzo por el aire, una gana de quedar y de subir al mismo tiempo: una inanidad de la pura pose después de cabeceo azul.

Como si se hubiera puesto a hervir el cielo en ese punto cada vez más pequeño.

Tanto que lo corrimos por el campo; tanto que los chicos nos corrieron a nosotros; tanto que sacaron la lengua, de rendidos, el Medor y el Lobo; que mortificamos a las vacas; que cortaron el cabestro los mansos; tanto...

The balloon they brought us from Buenos Aires, what a shame it left!

So much that the night before we prepared the ascent's string with as much ribbon as we could find dead or alive to make it a blue kite for the morning again.

It veered with the patio toward the side of the orange tree, gave its all through the air and brooked the light.

Did it go up?

It veered to the south where the reeds thin out and the chickens startle themselves all by themselves. We saw the all it gave, its will to both stay and rise: an absurdity of sheer posing after blue nodding.

As if the sky had set itself to boil in that steadily shrinking dot.

So much that we ran after it through the field; so much that the children ran after us; so much that their tongues lolled, exhausted, Medor and Wolf; that we tormented the cows; that the steer broke the reins; so much...

La lluvia de sobre techo y la lluvia de bajo techo cantan cantarán.

¡Ay, la gallina ya se entró cloqueando con las grandes alas de paraguas y este pío pío pasará pasará y el último quedará!

La cocina enloquecida como el arca, y nosotros y toda la lluvia tropezando con el Lobo echado extraordinariamente ante la puerta.

Se redondeaban las gotas en una torta frita, en dos, en fuente de amor de tortas fritas.

Saca tu cuaderno, saca tu pizarra, saca tu libro, saca la mano de aquí.

¡Que llueva, que llueva!

¡Se quemó la batata en el horno!

The on-the-roof rain and the under-the-roof rain sing will sing.

Oh, the chicken's already come in clucking with huge umbrella wings and this cheep-cheep will pass will pass and the last one will stay!

The kitchen crazy as the ark, and us and all the rain tripping over Wolf stretched out extraordinarily at the door.

The drops rounding themselves into a sweet little *torta frita*, into two *tortas fritas*, into a love fountain of *tortas fritas*.

Get your notebook, get your slate, get your book, stick your hand out.

It's raining! It's pouring!

We burned the sweet potato in the oven!

Al sol, al sol, al sol.

Las mil piernas del sol corriéndonos hasta este rincón de donde las calandrias vuelan a invitarlo a que juegue con nosotros.

Pero no hay que dejarse atrapar, no dejes los brazos sin correr, no te quedes quieta que te atrapará, te llevará.

La magulladura de cardo es también para mil piernas corriéndonos, corriéndonos hasta que nos pierden de vista bajo el aromo.

No saquen la cabeza, ni el pie. No saquen la mano, no sea que se ofenda el sol. No nos oiga el reír en el refugio: el aromo se quedará, ¡se quedaría!, sin su sombra.

To the sun, to the sun, to the sun.

The sun's thousand legs running us into this hollow where the calandra larks fly out to ask if he'll come play with us.

But don't let him catch you, don't stretch your arms out 'til you're running, don't just sit there or he'll catch you, he'll take you with him.

The bruise of the thistle too is for a thousand legs running, running us off to where they'll lose sight of us under the acacia tree.

Don't stick your head out, not even your feet out. Don't stick your hands out, don't do anything to upset the sun. Don't let him hear us laughing under cover: the acacia will stay, it would stay! without its shadow.

Rayuela canta en espiral con un pie en el suelo y el otro pie sin donde.

¡A llegar, a llegar!, y ya en el cielo de meollo bambolear la gracia, la vida entera. Y elijamos un cuadro con todos nuestros nombres y donde pararse una tarde momentito a descansar flamenco pata mansa.

Esa tarde que todos ganemos nos miraremos desde nuestros cuadros de descanso y sin pisar la raya.

Cuando la planta del pie no se llamará más, ni se llamará más pizarra, ni se llamará más llegamos en el recomienzo andará el solo pie de la tardecita pidiendo entrada y ya será de recomienzo mienzo.

Hacia afuera no está la palabra habrá caña dijo la araña.

El caracol más viejito ya no fresquea con los cuernos; a la punta de la loma tendrá que subirse antes de la noche y que subir con la loma a cuestas a la punta.

Luna de leche para terneros y niñales.

Hopscotch singing rounds with one foot on the ground and the other without anywhere.

Coming! coming! and already in the marrow sky, grace wobbling, life long. And let's pick a square with all our names to stand one little afternoon minute resting flamingo gentle foot.

That afternoon when we all win, we'll be watching each other from our resting squares and not stepping on the lines.

When the soles of your feet aren't named anymore, named pebble anymore, named all back at the beginning anymore, the only foot of the little late afternoon will go on begging entry and already all back at the beginning-ginning again.

The word isn't out there there will be wine said the vine.

The oldest little snail doesn't come out to cool off his horns anymore; he'll have to climb up to the top of the hill before night does and climb up to the top with the hill on his back.

Milk moon for calves and little-one-fields.

Con las compras y el pelo recién cortado, las alas del camino pavorreal subiéndonos en las cuatro ruedas de la vuelta.

El pabilo del poblado cada vez más pequeño, más allá abajo donde todas las luces se encendieron rápidamente a una. Y en cada esquina una sombra con su lucecita al lado; en cada zaguán con muchacha, la misma flor desde el flanco de su limpieza de lampazo.

Y ahora el auto que dice apurarse por el camino insolado de damas de noche; relente de campanada papá cerrando el día, leguas de loma entrando en el paso distraído, las tranqueras entornadas desde dentro hacia mañana. Campanada apúrense y floresta dentro de una vaca.

Volver con los ojos en blanco del mendigo,
con los ojos redondeados de la lechuza,
con los ojos del que nunca se miró en espejo,
con los ojos cerrados de la papa.

With parcels and new haircuts, the wings of the peacock road lifting us up onto the four wheels of our return.

The wick of the town smaller and smaller, down there where all the lights quickly kindled into one. And on every corner a shadow with its little light beside it; in every entryway, a girl, the same flowered silhouette bent into her mop.

And now the car that says hurry up along the road sun-struck with night jasmine; ringing bell mist papa closing the day, leagues of hills falling into distracted step, the half-closed gate from the inside toward morning. Hurry-up ringing bell and green glade in a cow.

>Come back with the beggar whites of your eyes,
>with rounded owl eyes,
>with never looked in a mirror eyes,
>with closed potato eyes.

Me lavé la cara en la luna nueva.

Toda en subida venía desde los eucaliptos, dejando su aseo al otoño sucio de quemarse. Y se le distrajo el iris en aquella subida con la luna hasta la casa una nochecita, y nos dimos vuelta para no dejarla demasiado atrás, mientras las niñas musitaban beruberu distraído con el labio. Cuando aún no acabábamos de atrasarnos oímos voces que se dirigían hacia nosotros. Cantaban. Eran los artistas del circo que todavía andaban a campo traviesa, ansiosos de más baile. Una armónica nos dijo que no tuviéramos miedo. La luna grande en medio, nos cruzamos mirándonos mirándonos.

Las muchachas casaderas se reían detrás del camino Real masticando flores de leche y una lucecita respondía en el bajo la primavera.

Allá se ve una luz, dijo el avestruz.

Adónde, dijo el conde.

Allá en la loma, dijo la paloma.

En aquel rancho, dijo el carancho.

Habrá baile, dijo el fraile.

Habrá vino, dijo el zorrino.

Habrá caña, dijo la araña.

I washed my face in the new moon.

Everything rising came up from the eucalyptus, showering clean ash autumn from the burn. And the iris distracted by the moon rising up to the house a little night, and we turned to be sure it wasn't too far behind while the girls murmured bababa distracted by their lips. We weren't done falling behind when we heard voices coming toward us. Singing. They were the circus folk still making their way through the field, eager for more dancing. The harmonica told us we needn't be afraid. The huge moon in the middle we ran into watching us, watching us.

The ladies laughing from behind the main road chewing the milk flowers and a little light whispered spring underneath.

Look! there's a light, said the mite.
Where, said the hare.
There on the hill, said the spoonbill.
In the pasture, said the aster.
There will be dance, said the cormorant.
There will be merry, said the berries.
There will be wine, said the vine.

El aire era de vidrio y estaba a punto de romperse. Unos subían vaso, otros alzaban botella, pero a la siesta no se la concluían.

Se hablaba casi como si no. La fiesta daba grandes voces al silencio punteado de caballos en el horizonte manso.

Las mujeres no decían ni de volverse ni de quedarse. Se ocuparon todas las sombras de los paraísos, y de allí se estiraba la voz como una pampa. Una bocha vino a quedar frente a nosotros, pifiada por la falta de impulso. A alguien le dio el mal y se la entró en las casas.

Una polvareda de tordos esperanzó con otro día, y el tuétano de sol pareció entibiarse. Los yuyos contra mis ojos brujulearon el vientito. Y hubo un desplazamiento a partir de los dos eucaliptos del frente donde estaban concentrados los hombres.

El recién venido era de una presencia firme, de unas ropas blancas y con una torcedura mayor de lo habitual en el ala del sombrero. Nosotros, que en ese momento jugábamos a la seta bayeta, nos pusimos a mirar para ese lado achicando los ojos.

Encargó que le abrieran la pista, que mientras galopaba por ella, alguien de la concurrencia le enlazara las dos manos a su malacara hasta rodar; él caería también en sus dos piernas y correría hasta la posta para ver de ganarle al animal otra vez en carrera.

Las mujeres alzaron a los niños más chicos para que pudieran ver.

Pero no. Tuvo miedo. Cuando pasó frente a nosotros los chiquilines, nos lo dijo casi sin dejar de silbar.

The air was glass and about to break. Some took up cup, others raised bottle, but no one slept that siesta.

They talked almost as if not. The party sent big voices into the silence punctured by horses along the steady horizon.

The women didn't say to come back or to stay either. They took up all the shade under the Paradise trees and stretched out their voices like a pampa. A ball stopped in front of us, done in by a lack of force. Someone got sick and went into one of the houses.

A dust cloud of cowbirds raised hopes with another day, and the sun's marrow seemed to cool. The grasses at my eyes followed after a light wind. And there was a shifting on the other side of the two eucalyptus where the men gathered.

The newcomer had a cool air, dressed in white, and with a particularly severe sprain in the brim of his hat. We, who were just then playing eeny meeny miny, looked aside lowering our eyes.

He had them open the ring, so that when he galloped in, someone from the crowd would lasso his horse's front hands and trip it hard down rolling, and he'd fall too on his own two legs and run as fast as he could to beat the animal back to the gate.

The women lifted the littlest children so they could see.

But no. He was scared. When he ran past us kids, he said so almost without whistling all the while.

Llegó la hora de las consejas mi madre.

Ya todos acostados, las ventanas abiertas a la loma aquietada; el verano.

Un ruido que no nos duerme del todo, alguien que va y que vuelve por el mismo retumbar del patio. Se da contra la azada que yo abandoné con su mordedura al yuyo.

Pero sigue, avanza, se pierde unos instantes y vuelve el enjaulado: nuestros pasos de pasmo sacados descalzos a la noche de granada.

Ni Lobo, y Medor, menos. Se les parece sin embargo como el gato montés a nuestros gatos dormilones.

Alguien dice la palabra. Noche de viernes.

Atiende, atiende con el oído, mi madre, las consejas de la noche.

The time has come for fables, mother.

All in bed and the windows opened to the quieted hill; summer.

A noise that keeps us from sleeping, someone who comes and goes with the same patio echo. Bumps into the hoe I left with its bite in the weeds.

But goes on, goes along, gets lost for a moment and comes back caged: our dazed steps off barefoot into the pomegranate night.

Not Wolf, and certainly not Medor. But it looks like them, the way the wild cat looks like our sleepy cats.

Someone says the word. Friday night.

Pay attention, pay attention with your ear, mother, night fables.

La loma de faldas anchas, entretenida con el niño, se olvida ahora de caerse rodando de sí misma.

Aprovecho el momento.

No nos está oyendo el diálogo y, por tanto, el tiempo se repite en una sílaba. Pero mi carta que se escribe frente a tu rostro inclinado en su biblia, le deja un lugar para luego de su juego retraído.

Aprovecho el momentito.

Cuando los dos lleguemos a recuento de lomas, a esquila de lana entera, no sería tan alegre.

Y no creo que la más parca de las rosas en su tallo sesgado, ni partir de pito de tren, ni la primera desnutrida de acacias, ni caerse de hojas en lo verde del viento, ni alegres años de la juventud de paso, ni la fundida de días y de noches del verano, entonen otra canción.

The wide skirt hill, distracted with the child, forgets now to fall down rolling.

This is my chance.

She can't hear us talking and, in as much, time repeats in a syllable. But my letter written with your face before it bent into its bible, leaves a space for later, after its slipping play away.

This is my little chance.

When we both arrive at the hills's counting, at the whole coat shearing, she won't be as happy.

And I don't think the most meager rose on its bending stem, or the train its leaving whistle, or the first barren of the acacia, or the leaves falling in the wind's green, or the happy years of a childhood passing, or the molten cast of summer days and nights, sing any other song.

Te pido que no te intranquilices, estoy tranquilo.
¿Es que viste alguna vez al bien y al mal separados?, ¿la escoria a muchas leguas de la rosa?
Ni Judas oscilante de amor colgado a su árbol en el no del amor sigue colgando.
¿Le diremos a la maleza que no suba?
¿A la maleza que no mienta pruebas en su favor y en su contra?
Ayer llovió y subió el cauce del arroyo y hoy bajó y en el atardecer el álamo del frente es la luz.
Yo te lo ruego.
Porque nadie puede disminuir el abrazo espejo ahora en el destiempo, el velar de madre en la lomada con las rodillas prontas y el morir de dios del hijo en el calor de falda desde adentro.

Please don't be worried, I'm not.

Is it that you once saw the good and bad apart from each other? the dross many leagues from the rose?

Not even love-pendulate Judas hung from his tree in the no-of-love is still hanging.

Should we tell the undergrowth not to rise?

The undergrowth not to plant evidence for or against itself?

Yesterday it rained and the riverbed filled up and today it went back down and by the afternoon the poplar out front is light.

I beg you.

Because no one can make smaller the now out-of-step mirror embrace, the mother's vigilant watch on the hill with readied knees and the son's dying god in the heat of her skirt from within.

Translator's Note

In August of 1959, Jorge Luis Borges and Adolfo Bioy Casares held in their hands a new book by a young poet from the northern pampas of Argentina who wore his gauchos and cowboy boots around Buenos Aires with a fierce, if soft-spoken, pride. The book, like its author, seemed to have floated in like a handful of seeds as tangible and familiar as they were palpably incipient and wild. *Cartas para que la alegría*, was, they agreed, "the title that bears all titles," a grammar that "leaves every window open." It was Arnaldo Calveyra's first book of poetry; it would also be the last printed in his homeland until the fall of the military dictatorship and its rule of state-sponsored terrorism in 1983.

Arnaldo Calveyra was born in 1929 in the remote hills of Mansilla, Entre Ríos province, to a farmer and rancher father (who died when he was very young), a mother who taught in the town primary school and twelve brothers and sisters. The language of the *campo*, the rich precision of the vocabulary of landscape and a uniquely truncated speech particular to the region, would be an essential guiding lens for Calveyra — both in terms of experience and expression — throughout the rest of his life. In 1950, he left to study at the Faculty of Humanities at the National University of La Plata, about 50 miles south of Buenos Aires, where he would meet Carlos Mastronardi who became not only a mentor, but very much a father figure to Calveyra. Perhaps it is not uncommon to think of Argentina's troubled political landscape as beginning in the 1970s with what is known as the

Dirty War (a controversial term I use reluctantly for historical context here) but the roots of those years of horrific state violence extend far back into the annals of the country's history. Calveyra had come of age in a time of extreme political turmoil and, along with most of his fellow students and the intellectual left, vehemently opposed the 1943 military coup and Axis-sympathizing military regime that saw the rise to power of Colonel Juan Perón. As Perón's authoritarian regime metastasized into the 1950s, Calveyra and other intellectuals who refused to become members of the Peronist party were subsequently prevented from their teaching posts and any work tantamount to their education and training. Forced to take work as a pest control exterminator, Calveyra and his fellow young writers and students continued nevertheless to write and gather in the cafes of Buenos Aires and La Plata — pooling their meager handfuls of money to hire back their former professors (equally ousted from their academic positions and replaced with Peronist supporters) for informal lectures and workshops. One of those lecturers was Jorge Luis Borges, with whom Calveyra spent many long and nutritive afternoons. But it was Carlos Mastronardi who was Calveyra's greatest teacher; Calveyra travelled every weekend for almost ten years to Mastronardi's home in Buenos Aires where they would walk for hours in the evenings talking poetry and language and politics. It was Mastronardi who, in 1959, introduced Calveyra to the publisher of his first book *Cartas para que la alegría*, and Mastronardi too who, along with writer and publisher of the famed *Sur* magazine Victoria Ocampo, would arrange for Calveyra to travel to Paris the following year.

Calveyra's trip to Paris in 1960 would prove to be the first leg of a two-part journey that would end in permanent exile. In Paris, he would meet and deeply impress Gaëtan Picon (essayist, critic and Director-General of Art and Letters) who would offer him a research fellowship to stay in Europe. Calveyra, feeling the tug of his family and homeland, initially turned down the offer and returned to Argentina. But the 1950s and 60s in Argentina were marked with frequent coups d'état and the winds had shifted again upon Calveyra's return; the political atmosphere seemed to be growing more sinister and Calveyra's prospects as a young intellectual felt decidedly dark. By a stroke of good fortune, Picon had not given up on Calveyra and had sent a second offer from the French Ministry by post; it was an offer the young writer who was as invigorated by Paris's culture of the arts as he was uncertain about his own future in Argentina's turbulent authoritarian landscape, could not refuse. In 1961, Calveyra left Argentina on an Arts and Letters research fellowship. By the mid-1970s, he was warned not to return to Argentina — the intellectual left was being systematically targeted by right-wing death squads. (In the summer of 1983, Calveyra returned to Argentina for the first time since 1961 where he was targeted by a death squad and narrowly escaped to Uruguay with the help of the French Consulate.)

While the circumstances around Calveyra's sustained exile from Argentina were deeply painful — particularly leaving his mother whom he would never see again —, his journey to Paris also marked the beginning of a joyful adult life as a poet and artist surrounded by friends and comrades who would become his lifetime community. It is in Paris that Calveyra would meet both his future wife Monique Tur and dearest friend Julio Cortázar. Cortázar, along with Alejandra Pizarnik, Italo Calvino, Aurora Bernárdez, Julio Silva, Claude Roy, Antoine Vitez, Saúl Yurkievich, Hugo Santiago, Eduardo Jonquières, Rodolfo Nieto, and Peter Brook, as well as exiles who came later in the 70s like Juan José Saer and Lautaro Murúa and others who comprised this particular group of writers and artists moving between Paris and Saignon in Provence, would become Calveyra's new family in his new homeland. Cortázar and Calveyra became particularly close and developed a steady and intimate correspondence (usually delivered by hand or tucked into each other's doorframes) that nourished both men deeply until Cortázar's premature passing in 1984.

Unsurprisingly, Calveyra eventually grew to be a vastly influential poet in France; in 1999, he was awarded France's highest national medal for contributions to the arts — Commander of the French Order of Arts and Letters. Laure Bataillon, writer and translator, and fellow traveler of Calveyra's circle of friends, began translating Calveyra's works into French in 1969 and would continue to do so until her passing in 1990. Over the course of his lifetime, Calveyra received multiple honors and awards for his work in France, including both the Chevalier and Officier national medals as well, but did not really begin gaining recognition in his own country until the 1990s once the political atmosphere in Argentina had shifted enough to allow for the return and celebration of exiled voices.

In the poem "Maizal del Gregoriano," Calveyra writes, "Don't forget to be in many places at once, lightly at times, other times ubiquitously (...) It doesn't matter how. The important thing is not to forget, not to forget oneself," not to forget "the power of forgetting" and "the different kinds of forgetting." Calveyra did not forget Entre Ríos. He used to say that when he opened his window in Paris he saw two horizons, not superimposed, but not discrete either — he called this his "double horizon." Calveyra was radial in the geometries of his being and just as much in his work — his was a state of suspended light, of the slippery conspiracies of the material and the sensory, of distances and depths brought near enough to touch but with the tender cognizance that touch itself was elusive. What captivated Borges and Mastronardi in 1959 was Calveyra's singular use of syntax and language. It is often said that Calveyra invented a new grammar that could release time and place from the stasis and confinement that words inescapably mark. Calveyra refused this recognition, "What I wanted to do with *Cartas para que la alegría* was recover the colloquial language of the people of the campo (...) I invented nothing, rather the people actually spoke this way, *de una manera cifrada*" (*cifrada* here meaning both "reduced to the essence" and "encrypted"). *Cartas* is the story of Calveyra leaving Entre Ríos as a young man for Buenos Aires, leaving the landscape and people he loved but that could not contain him — it reads as if written already from a place of exile, and in many ways it was. Calveyra used to say that he spent his lifetime writing the same book — a book of dispersion and through dispersion, preservation.

In some ways, perhaps, translation is another leg in this journey of distances — to near by way of distance, to identify by obscurity, to be in many places at once, and at once, remember the many kinds of forgetting — dispersion and through dispersion, preservation. In this translation I have sought to preserve the otherness of the *Cartas* landscape — that singular syntax and lexis borne from the "essential" precision and uniquely encrypted speech of the Entre Ríos landscape — while just as much maintaining the familiarity and ease of the inviting momentum of the original. One example of note is the way in which Calveyra peppers the poems in *Cartas* with the language of Argentine nursery rhymes such that the scene momentarily obfuscates and shifts from sensory to memory before falling back into the particulars of the Entre Ríos lexis and landscape. In the English translation, I have chosen to use American nursery rhymes, as did Laure Bataillon in the French, in order to give the reader that same sense of unexpected disorientation and yet simultaneous familiarity and trust — discovery by a mechanic of memory.

In the unique and diffuse grammar that is Calveyra's voice, a clause can at any moment turn noun turn adjective turn gerund turn dangling participle turn complete sentence (a list whose order is interchangeable). And yet at the same time, Calveyra's is nevertheless a very vivid and graspable prose; any unexpected abstraction of syntax is always to beget clarity, and so must both momentarily obfuscate and simultaneously clarify in the English as well. Calveyra's poems are rich and playful with occasional end rhyme, slant and internal rhyme, and dilating repetition. Together with his toppling syntactical style — propelling sentences through front-ended dependent clauses or adjectival phrases, forwarding objects to the fronts of sentences while sustaining the active voice, a latent anapestic tetrameter, and the propulsive stringing of "and ... and ... and" that drives the reader near-breathless through many of the book's pages — the rhythm of *Cartas* is one of somersaulting, if gentle, itinerancy. While the Spanish language may front-load clauses somewhat more frequently than English, Calveyra's repetition of this structure, and particularly inverting syntax such that sentences remain active yet begin with direct or indirect objects, is unusual even to the Spanish, or Argentine, ear. And yet, according to Calveyra, the structure and sound of this capsizing grammar is natural to the "essential" speech of the people of the Entre Ríos region/time he grew up in; as if his mother tongue were from the very beginning a prose of propulsion. Perhaps he heard this same rhythm in the gaining steam of the train's wheels as they chugged down the track that fateful morning he left Mansilla — the train Calveyra tells us he is on in the very first poem, the one that would carry him to Buenos Aires and then La Plata and then Paris, forever. "Pay attention, pay attention with your ear, mother, night fables."

I had the great honor of meeting Arnaldo Calveyra in 2010 at a poetry festival in Spain. It is a rare thing to meet a writer whose being and writing plait by the same breath, but Arnaldo was that rare thing — he was as diffuse and intense and deeply loving in his being as any poem he'd ever written. He whispered and watched and listened just as he wrote and read and remembered. It is only a testament to Arnaldo's limitless embrace that he was willing to take me, a young poet and translator, under his wing. After that week in Córdoba, we developed a faithful correspondence — written in Word, attached to email — ; his letters lifted up off the screen like diffuse molecules evaporating as they formed. Meanwhile I was reading and re-reading his every work I could find and inevitably one day asked if he might be willing to permit me try to translate one of his books of poetry into English. If this translation has succeeded in any small way, it is because of Arnaldo's generous commitment to this project, his tireless and patient explanations and anecdotes, and the many hours he leant to working on the manuscript together.

After Arnaldo passed away in January of 2015, it took me some time to look at *Cartas* again. It was in 2016, when Emmalea Russo of Ugly Duckling Presse contacted me about its publication, that I finally opened my emails from Arnaldo again, looking for contacts for his family. So it was that by some stroke of "the winds that travel from a sadness to a happiness," that I would quickly discover that Arnaldo's son Beltran, himself a writer, happened to be living in New York for the year. Needless to say, it was a friendship begun long before we met. This publication would not be possible without the inimitable insight and support of Beltran Calveyra — his indefatigable dedication to the editing of this manuscript and endless afternoons of recounting his father's biography for my eager notes. I am indebted too to the Argentine poet and translator Silvina López Medin, who with exacting and generous insight, has helped answer any remaining question marks about the translation, expertly identifying elements of the Argentine-specific landscape and nuances of the Entre Ríos dialect. Thank you to Emmalea Russo, Daniel Owen, Kyra Simone, Harris Bauer, Matvei Yankelevich, Anna Moschovakis and all of the UDP collective for bringing Arnaldo Calveyra, his voice and his work, to English-language readers at last. And finally, above all, thank you to Monique Tur, for her gentle and steadfast encouragement from the very beginning.

About the Author

Argentine poet and playwright Arnaldo Calveyra (1929-2015) is considered a national treasure both in his adopted country of France and homeland of Argentina. Exiled to Paris in 1961, Calveyra wrote and published the vast majority of his works in that country (translated into the French by Laure Bataillon among others) and was the recipient of multiple national honors in his lifetime including, in 1999, France's highest award for contribution to the arts and literature —the national medal *Commandeur des Arts et des Lettres.*

Born in 1929, Calveyra came of age during a time of political turmoil in Argentina characterized by frequent coups d'état. The Axis-sympathizing military coup of 1943 saw the rise to power of Colonel Juan Perón, whom Calveyra opposed and whose authoritarian regime would prevent Calveyra (who refused to become a member of the Peronist party) from acquiring a teaching post or any work tantamount to his education. Forced to take work as a pest control exterminator, Calveyra and his fellow young poets continued to meet in the cafes of Buenos Aires and La Plata with their former professors (also ousted from their academic positions) including Jorge Luis Borges, Adolfo Bioy Casares and Carlos Mastronardi. In 1960, after the publication of Calveyra's celebrated first book of poetry *Cartas para que la alegría*, Mastronardi and editor Victoria Ocampo arranged for the young poet to travel to Paris where he would meet the Director-General of Art and Letters, Gaëtan Picon. A year later, Calveyra received an offer from Picon to return to Paris on a research fellowship, an offer the young writer who was as invigorated by Paris's culture of the arts as he was uncertain about his own future in Argentina's turbulent authoritarian landscape, could not refuse. By the mid-1970s, Calveyra was warned not to return to Argentina — the intellectual left was being systematically targeted by right-wing death squads. In Paris, Calveyra would meet both his future wife Monique Tur and dearest friend Julio Cortázar. Cortázar, along with Italo Calvino, Antoine Vitez, Hugo Santiago, Rodolfo Nieto and Peter Brook, among others, would become Calveyra's new family in his new homeland. Calveyra and Monique Tur were married in 1968 and had two children, Beltran and Eva; Calveyra would live in Paris until his passing in 2015.

Following the fall of the military dictatorship in 1983, Calveyra's work was slowly recovered in Argentina; in 1988, poet Juan Gelman recommended Calveyra to the Argentine publisher Jose Luis Mangieri, effectively reintroducing him to an Argentine audience. The author of over 25 works of literature and theater, Calveyra's major works include *Cartas para que la alegría* (poetry), *El diputado está triste* (theater), *Latin American Trip* (theater), *Iguana, iguana* (poetry), *Maizal del gregoriano* (poetry), *El origen de la luz* (fiction), *El hombre del Luxemburgo* (poetry), *Si la Argentina fuera una novela* (essay), *Diario del fumigador de guardia* (poetry), *Diario de Eleusis* (poetry), and the posthumously published *Diario Francés* (poetry).

Photograph by Grete Stern

Acknowledgments

Excerpts from *Letters So That Happiness* first appeared in *Conjunctions 59* and *Washington Square Review*. Many thanks to the editors.